HOW
TO
BE
AN
INVENTOR

Also by Harvey Weiss

Harvey Weiss

HOW TO BE AN INVENTOR

Illustrated with photographs and drawings by the author

HarperCollins*Publishers*

Thanks and acknowledgements are due the following organizations, who granted permission to reproduce material from their collections: The Biblioteca Ambrosiana, Milan, Italy, for the drawings by Leonardo da Vinci on pages 44 and 45; The Royal Library, England, for the drawing by Leonardo da Vinci on page 73; The National Archives, Washington, D.C., for the photographs and drawings on pages 25, 27, 67, 71, 78, and 79; The Greenfield Village and Henry Ford Museum, Dearborn, Michigan, for the photograph on page 11; King Features Syndicate, New York, N.Y., for the cartoons on pages 83 and 84; The New York Public Library, New York, N.Y., for the drawing on page 42; The IBM Corporation, Armonk, N.Y., for the photographs on pages 9, 74, and 75; The Museum of Modern Art, Stockholm, Sweden, for the photograph on page 33. The musical instrument on page 65 was made by Victor de Santi. The models on pages 15, 16, 32, 34, 38, 86, 87, 90, 92, and 93 are by the author.

How to Be an Inventor
Copyright © 1980 by Harvey Weiss

Library of Congress Cataloging-in-Publication Data

Weiss, Harvey.
  How to be an inventor.

  SUMMARY: Discusses different types of inventors
and their creations and gives advice on becoming an
inventor.
  1. Inventions—Juvenile literature. [1. Inventions]
I. Title.
T339.W42   608   79–7823
ISBN 0–690–04052–0
ISBN 0–690–04053–9 (lib. bdg.)

3 4 5 6 7 8 9 10

Contents

What Is an Invention?

An invention is something new or original—something made up, something that never existed until the inventor thought it up.

You could say that a poem, a story, a painting, or a song is an invention. It is, in its own way, and a poet or composer or painter might be called an inventor. People refer to the *art* of invention. Perhaps they do this because there is a similarity between the creative artistic process and the kind of invention this book is all about.

There are many different kinds of inventors—more or less artistic; more or less practical; more or less creative. They are discussed in the next few pages in more detail. But there is one kind of inventor that this book isn't really about or for, and that is the scientist-inventor, the expert who has a lot of knowledge and experience in a technical field. The kinds of inventions this book is about require only common sense and imagination and a willingness to give even a farfetched idea some kind of a try.

Most inventions are practical. They try to simplify a task or accomplish useful work. But the kind of invention many amateur inventors like best is the kind made just for the fun of it. It may be impractical and even completely useless, but it is fun to dream up and put together, and good to have around when it is completed.

This is a model of an invention by the great sixteenth-century artist, Leonardo da Vinci. It is a wire-testing device. One end of the wire to be tested is attached to the beam at the top. The other end is attached to the basket. The large container with the chute at the bottom is filled with sand. A little door at the end of the chute is held open by the chains holding the basket. Sand pours out of the chute into the basket, finally breaking the wire as the weight of the sand increases. The basket falls, in turn causing the door of the chute to close. Then, by weighing the basket, the strength of the wire can be determined. This model wasn't built by da Vinci himself. It is a modern construction that was put together from drawings da Vinci made. Several more da Vinci drawings and models are illustrated elsewhere in this book.

Why Invent Anything?

There are different kinds of inventors, and they have different reasons for wanting to invent. If we take a look at some of these various types, we will get a better idea of what this business of inventing is all about.

Fame and Fortune

Many people have fame and fortune in mind when they think about inventing. And why not? Who doesn't want to become rich and famous? It would be nice to sell an idea to a large corporation for two million dollars; or to invent a chemical that you could put in the gas tank of a car so that the engine would run on water; or to figure out a way to change brass into gold. You could sell for a great deal of money a machine that used

This is a model N Ford. Like many inventions it was a combination of other designs that had already been developed. What Henry Ford really invented was a system for manufacturing something on a large scale in an efficient, economical way. And in the process he became a very rich and famous person.

air for fuel, or a perpetual-motion machine, or a bar of soap that would never dissolve.

Actually, some simple inventions *have* made their inventors wealthy. For example, a man by the name of William Hunt invented the safety pin in 1849 and made a fortune. Another simple device, the safety razor, was invented by E. C. Gillette, who became a millionaire. And we all know about people like Henry Ford, Thomas Edison, and Eli Whitney, whose inventions brought them fame and fortune.

About a hundred years ago another inventor, whose name we don't know, thought he would become rich and famous with the "swimming device" shown here in an old illustration. The swimmer was supposed to sit on a battery-powered electric motor that turned a propeller. The device would propel the wearer through the water in comfort and with speed—if he didn't sink first! (Or if he wasn't electrocuted.) This is one inventor who may have had a lot of fun developing his idea—but we can be quite certain it didn't make him very rich or famous.

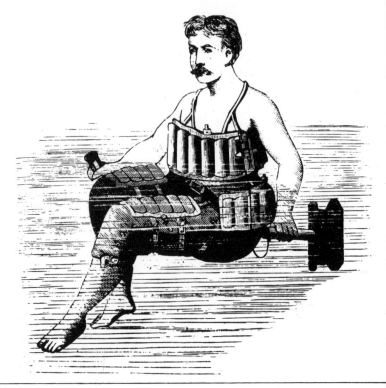

The Scientist–Inventor

This category is probably the largest and the people in it the most serious. These inventors are real experts, with training and experience, and with lots of workshop equipment and tools at their disposal. They often work for large corporations. Organizations like the Bell Telephone Company, the automobile companies, and General Electric have large staffs of people continually working on new inventions, which will be included in or among the products they manufacture and sell.

This sort of inventor is a professional—a scientist, really—and it is his or her *job* to invent. This kind of inventing is often called "research," and it is much too complicated and sophisticated for us to concern ourselves with. And besides, amateur inventors don't have to answer to a boss.

The Practical Inventor

There is the inventor who has a problem and sets about finding a solution for it. This is the practical inventor. Below is a practical device that has been invented many times over by thousands of people. The problem is that the dog (or cat) is always scratching to get in or out the back door. The solution is to make a small swinging door that is set into the large door. If the "pet door" is hinged on top, the dog (or cat) can come and go as it pleases. The little door will swing closed after the animal has passed. (Maybe you can invent a way to keep the fleas out!)

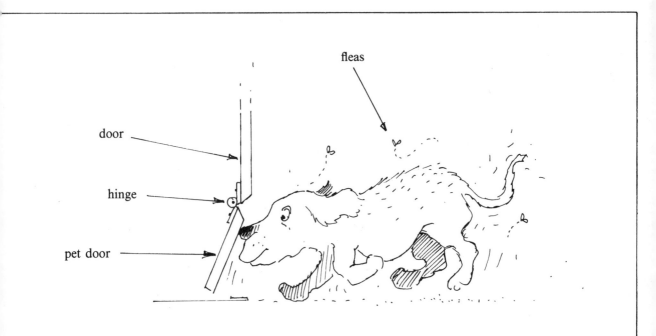

The Inventor–Inventor

There is a kind of inventor who wants to invent something
—anything—simply because he or she is fascinated by the
entire idea of inventing! The *process* of inventing is what is most
important. It is great fun to think of something, draw the plans,
and build a model, get it to work, and show it to one's friends.
And this is worth doing even if the invention is not terribly
practical, or is even downright useless. It is a way of saying,
"I'm something special. I'm an inventor. I have contributed
this *thing* to the world. It didn't exist—never was—until I
came along and invented it."

The steam-propelled model airplane shown on the opposite
page is the sort of thing an inventor–inventor might invent. It
isn't practical, though it does work in its own clumsy way. The
model was expensive and difficult to build. It took a lot of time

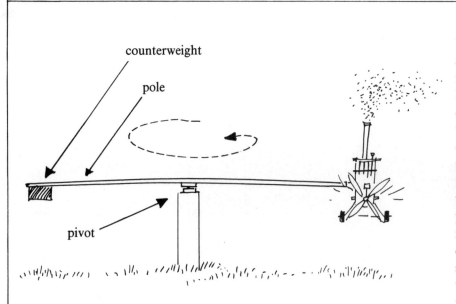

counterweight

pole

pivot

This overweight model
airplane could obviously
never get off the ground.
But it can be placed at one
end of a twelve-foot pole,
with a counterweight at the
other end of the pole and a
pivot in the center. When
the boiler is fired up and
the engine gets going, the
propeller turns at a great
rate and the entire
cumbersome apparatus
slowly circles around—in
the manner of a wheezy
merry-go-round.

Here is a device that requires a certain amount of woodworking skill. It isn't a new invention by any means. It is simply a variation of the mechanism that makes clocks tick. It is called an escapement. As the weight on the string sinks lower and lower, it causes the large, toothed, horizontal wheel to turn. The speed at which the wheel turns is controlled by two little metal "fingers," which are connected to the long, swinging pendulum. You can make a similar device as an interesting and handsome decoration or as a mechanical exercise.

to build. But in the eyes of the inventor (who also happens to be the author of this book), it is a very beautiful *thing,* and all his friends admire it (they *have* to admire it if they want to remain his friends) and it was well worth the time and trouble it took.

The Builder–Inventor

Many people like the process of building things. The operation of sawing, filing, fitting together, attaching gears and levers and counterweights—all the bits and pieces of the mechanical and electrical arts—can be enormously appealing. It is the business of putting things together rather than the end result that is most interesting to the builder–inventor. If he or she can assemble an invention and get it to work, that is satisfaction enough.

Although five separate types of inventors are listed here, there is obviously going to be a lot of overlapping. Almost everybody likes the idea of creating something new, and certainly nobody ignores the odd chance of hitting it rich with a sensational new idea.

This book isn't about any one particular kind of inventor or invention. It is more about the ways ideas for inventions come into being, and about how these ideas are developed. The sort of invention you are likely to come up with will depend on what you are interested in and what you know something about.

Here's another invention—somebody's bright idea—that never quite succeeded. It is called "an apparatus to prevent snoring." It seems as if the leather straps, a sort of harness, are intended to keep the mouth from opening, thus preventing snoring. Actually the invention might really work. The straps would probably be so uncomfortable the wearer couldn't fall asleep —in which case he wouldn't snore!

How to
Go About It

In this chapter we'll discuss the different ways of getting started —how you come up with an idea for an invention. There are many approaches, depending on what sort of inventor you are, or would like to be, and what your interests are. You may, in fact, already have some bright idea for an invention and be impatient to get on with it. In this case you have a head start, and after reading this chapter you can quickly get on with drawing plans and making a working model.

For hundreds of years inventors have struggled with the challenge of flying. One inventor in the 1800s devised the flying machine shown here. The wings, constructed of wood and silk, were designed to imitate a bat's wings. The inventor and his machine were lifted to a height of several hundred feet by means of a hot air balloon. Then he was released and tried to fly gracefully down to earth. Unfortunately the apparatus didn't work very well, and the inventor didn't survive the experiment.

Brainstorming

As we have said in the previous chapter, many inventors are trying to solve a problem—perhaps how to get a kite to fly in a light breeze; how to make sure an egg cooks for only three minutes so that it will be perfectly soft-boiled; how to turn off the bedroom lights when you are already in bed; how to get a bicycle to coast uphill. These are the sort of problems the practical inventor might be concerned with.

Let's take an example of a problem and see how you might go about solving it. Suppose you live in a house in the country and it is your job to take the garbage out. Every night after supper you have to carry the garbage to the can, which is kept fifty yards away, by the back fence. This is a very annoying job when the weather is bad. The problem, then, is how to get the garbage from the back door to the garbageman—who incidentally comes every day—without having to travel the fifty yards. (The obvious solution to this problem is to move the garbage can closer, right outside the back door. But this won't work because the garbage man wants the can close to where he stops his truck, and that is fifty yards away, by the back fence.)

The method to use—the inventor's method—is to think of as many solutions as you can. Perhaps an impractical or even silly possibility will suggest something else that is workable. The trick is to get a piece of paper and write down *all* possibilities as they occur to you. Here are some ideas that you might think of:

1. Wrap the garbage into a tight package, stand at the back door, and throw the package into the garbage can.
2. Train the dog to pick up the package of garbage and carry it out.
3. Save the garbage for a warm, sunny day when you won't mind taking it out.
4. Don't eat, so there won't be any garbage.
5. Figure out a way to move the garbage can back and forth so that you can just lean out the door and drop the garbage in.
6. Build a cable car or a derrick that can carry the garbage to the can.
7. Make a giant slingshot that will shoot the garbage into the can.

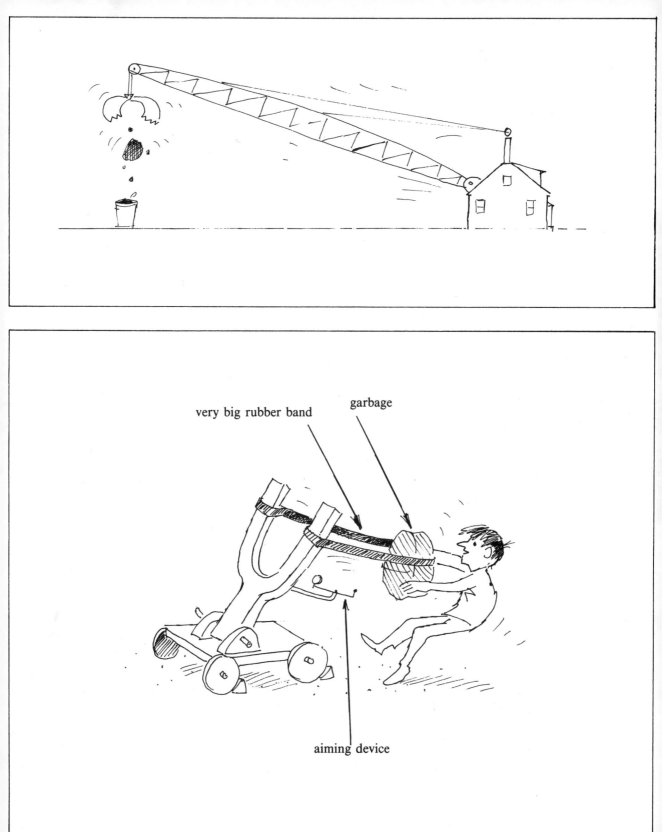

very big rubber band

garbage

aiming device

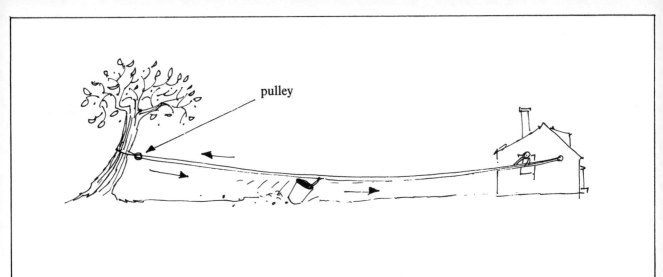

pulley

8. Don't use a can. Put the garbage into a disposable plastic bag, form it into a nice, tight ball, and roll it into a garbage collecting corner by the fence.
9. Bypass the garbage man. Dig a big hole outside the kitchen window, dump the garbage into it, and cover it over with dirt.

Some of these possibilities are obviously ridiculous. But you might decide that number five has the germ of an idea. How about if the garbage can was put on wheels and you rigged up a rope and pulleys so you could pull the can to the back door, and then, after the garbage was loaded, pull it back out to the back fence? Eureka! It will work. You've invented a moving garbage can—a great new technical breakthrough in garbage disposal systems! And that's how it goes. . . .

pulley

This process of writing down a long list of all possible (and impossible) solutions to a problem is called brainstorming. It is a very effective method that often produces original and workable ideas.

After all, you can't simply sit around staring into space waiting for an inspiration—you may wait forever! You must get your mind working. And the brainstorming way is a good way to do it.

The brainstorming method will work for one person alone, or for two or more people. But in any case you must write down *all* ideas or possibilities, as many as you can think of. And you must be sure never to laugh at or sneer at or ignore any suggestion that seems farfetched, silly, or just plain dumb. If you were to do that, you would make yourself, or anyone else, self-conscious and inhibited, which might well close off the free flow of imaginative ideas. Remember that often an impractical idea will lead to or suggest a workable idea.

Changes and Improvements

Very few inventions just pop up with no connection to anything else. Henry Ford's automobile was simply an improved version of other, earlier designs. Many inventors had experimented with airplane designs before the Wright brothers managed their first powered flight in 1903.

The "changed" or "improved" invention often grows out of personal experience. If you regularly do some sort of routine task and suddenly think of a way to speed up or simplify it, you will probably have come up with an invention of some practical value. Suppose, for example, you had to sharpen hundreds of pencils with a hand-cranked pencil sharpener. With some

thought (perhaps after a brainstorming session), you might come up with the idea of attaching a steam engine to the sharpener. This would be a practical and worthwhile improvement to an already existing invention. (Someone has already come up with a similar invention, of course. In any large stationery store you will find a variety of automatic, electric-powered pencil sharpeners.)

Here is a rather bloodthirsty invention that is a change and an "improvement." It is simply a combination of two separate things—a knife and a revolver. Neither the knife nor the revolver was new when this invention was patented in 1837. But by combining the two, something new—if useless—was invented.

This is another invention that simply combines two already existing parts—a bicycle-type pedal arrangement and a large fan blade. It is a sort of man-powered helicopter and would be lots more fun than a bicycle—if only it would work!

There was a fellow by the name of J. C. Boyle who, we can guess, was a very proper gentleman who greeted all his lady friends by tipping his hat. (In the 1890s this was a usual, well-bred form of greeting.) He must have had a lot of lady friends, or thought that other gentlemen who were tired of excessive hat-tipping would be interested in his invention, because he patented the device shown opposite.

The patent was issued on March 10, 1896. The drawing isn't very clear, but it seems that there is some kind of mechanism that will raise the front part of the hat. Boyle didn't invent the hat. He didn't invent the mechanical arrangement that tilted the hat. What he did do was combine a few already existing parts to get the kind of action he wanted.

J. C. BOYLE.
SALUTING DEVICE.

No. 556,248.

Patented Mar. 10, 1896.

Fig: 1.

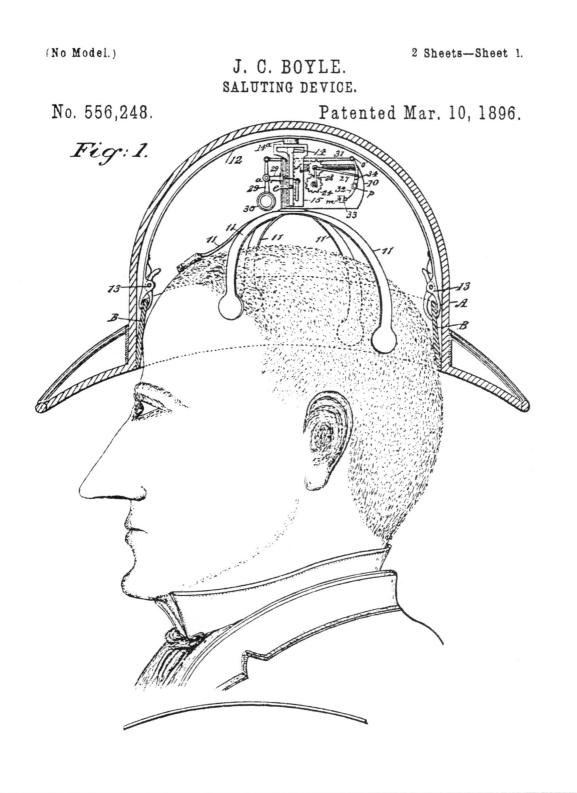

Observation

There is the much-told story of how James Watt invented the steam engine. It is said that he noticed that water boiling in his teakettle produced steam that jiggled the lid of the kettle. From this observation he reasoned that steam was capable of doing work. If a small kettle of boiling water could make enough steam to move the kettle lid, a lot of steam from a large boiler could really do some useful work.

This story of Watt and the teakettle is not a true story. Various kinds of steam engines were being used before Watt was born. Watt changed and improved an idea that others had already worked on. But the story does make the point that new ideas come about from observing and thinking about common everyday occurrences.

If you are alert, observant, curious, you will no doubt notice all kinds of things happening about you all the time that may give you ideas for inventions. For example, you might notice a piece of paper fluttering in the air rising above a hot radiator. And that might give you some ideas for hot-air engines. Or you may have seen water rising and falling as the tides come and go. Isn't this a source of power worth thinking about?

Inventing with Odds and Ends

There is a type of invention that grows out of the junk box. Most households have a place where leftover bits and pieces are kept. It may be an odd kitchen drawer where things collect, or a carton in the basement, or a box tucked away at the back of a closet shelf. It's the place where discarded tools or parts of old machinery are put away. This is where broken clocks and old eyeglasses end up. It is the last resting place for rusty roller-skate wheels, odd gears, bicycle parts, electric light sockets, wire, springs, pulleys, spools, lenses, nails and nuts and bolts, hooks, cracked pencil sharpeners, and so on.

When an amateur inventor in search of an idea starts rummaging around in such a "treasure chest," various possibilities will usually suggest themselves.

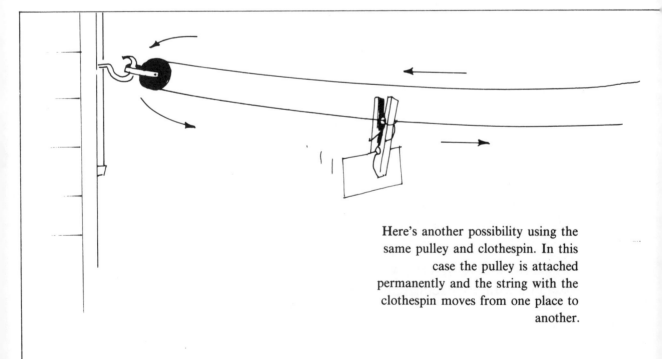

This method of inventing is putting the cart before the horse. You might come up with some sort of gadget or combination of parts, and *then* try to find a way of using it. (In a sense you would be finding the solution first, then finding the problem it solves!)

Let's take an example. Suppose, while rummaging around in your junk box, you came upon a small pulley, a spring clothespin, and a ball of string. After a little thought—or some brainstorming—you might think of a message delivery device! You could attach the clothespin to the pulley. Then you could put

Here's another possibility using the same pulley and clothespin. In this case the pulley is attached permanently and the string with the clothespin moves from one place to another.

the pulley on the string, which you would stretch from a high point in one room to a low point in another room (or out the window to some faraway location). Now you can write a message on a slip of paper, attach it to the clothespin, and let the pulley slide along the string and down to the recipient at the other end.

Inventing out of the junk box can produce some very odd things with no practical purpose at all. Suppose you found a paintbrush and some wood strips and nuts and bolts and invented a *revolving brush!* It might be quite interesting to put together, but then what would you use it for? Painting polka dots? Cleaning glasses? Tickling pussycats? Generating static electricity on balloons? Spattering paint?

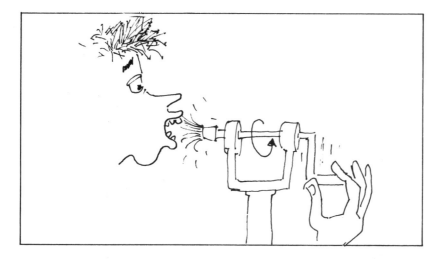

If you like the way your invention looks, or the way it moves, or the conversation that it generates, that may be reason enough for having put it together. Let your friends figure out for themselves what it is supposed to do!

There is a man by the name of Jean Tinguely who makes machines with no practical purpose. Only he doesn't call them machines. They are called art, or sculpture, rather than machinery, and they are exhibited in museums and art galleries and are bought by art collectors for a great deal of money. The sculpture (or is it an invention?) on the opposite page is by Jean Tinguely. It is a motor-driven device that operates a marker pen that draws on a roll of paper. Some of the parts in this sculpture–machine serve a practical purpose, moving the pen and feeding out the paper. Other parts are included simply because they help to make a good-looking design.

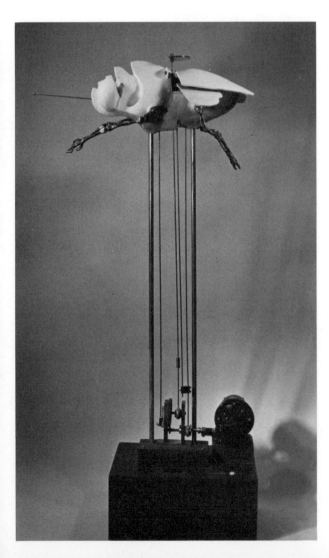

The ladybug shown here is another sculpture–invention. The wings and antenna on this oversize insect wiggle about in a somewhat lifelike fashion when the gearing system is put into motion. An electric motor is started by pressing a button. The gears turn and the long brass rods move up and down, working the various levers inside the body of the bug, which are in turn connected to the wings and antenna. This sort of construction requires the skill of both the sculptor and the inventor–mechanic. In this case the gears and cams have been left in plain sight on top of the base because they are as attractive and interesting to watch in motion as the ladybug itself.

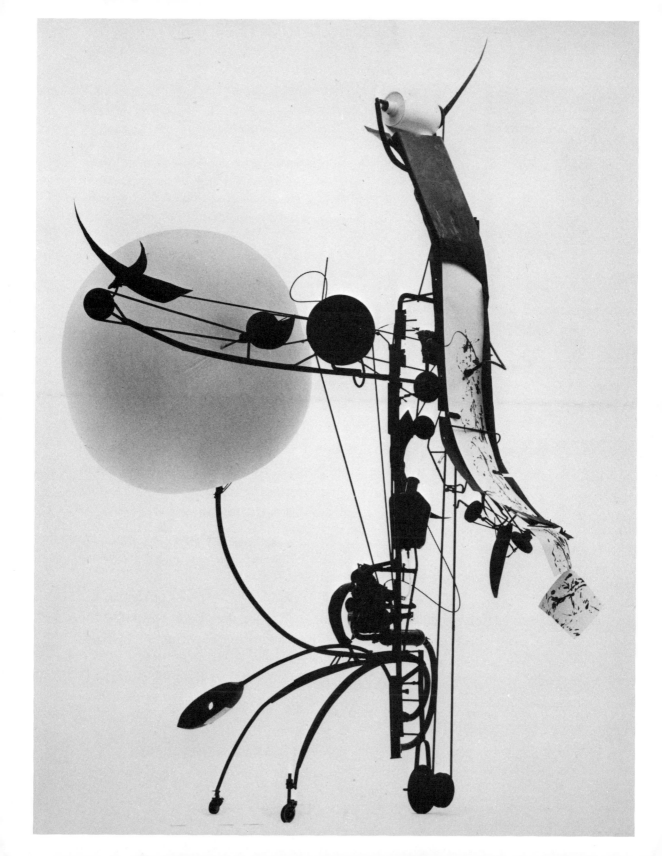

This fancy-free car-boat-plane is really more an excuse for making an offbeat wood model than a serious, practical design for an invention. This vehicle has the wings and propeller of an airplane, the hull and propeller of a boat, and wheels like those of a car for traveling on land. It is supposed to be propelled by a steam engine—why not?—and you can see the top of the boiler and the smokestack sticking up in front of the upper wing. It looks a little like the invention shown on page 6.

Some areas of exploration are not very suitable for the amateur inventor. Chemistry, for example, is one of them. This is a fascinating science, but unless the inventor really understands what it is all about, there is not much he or she can expect to accomplish. There is no point in simply mixing chemicals and hoping for something interesting to happen. The interesting thing might be an explosion or poisonous vapors! There are, of course, all kinds of chemistry experiments one can perform. These are described in textbooks and laboratory manuals, and they are not really inventions.

Biology, aeronautics, and electronics are other fields that are rather difficult for the amateur unless he or she has had some training and experience. Besides, many experiments in these areas stretch over long periods of time.

Models
and Drawings

Getting a marvelous idea for an invention is the most important thing. And sometimes you will be satisfied with simply thinking about your invention, imagining how well it would solve a problem, and letting it go at that. At other times, though, you will want to draw up plans to illustrate exactly how your invention works, or make an actual model of the invention. After all, the United States Department of Defense is not going to buy your idea for a flying submarine (a flubmarine?) unless you can show them a drawing or a model that will demonstrate to them its many virtues.

Of course, there will be times when you may have no need for drawings and models—if you don't plan to sell your idea to the government, or if your invention isn't unusually large, or when you know exactly how you want it to be. Then you can just go ahead and put the thing together and that's that.

Models

One reason for making a model is to show in small scale how some bulky device would look and work if actually built. For example, if you had an idea for a new kind of airplane wing for a transport plane, you wouldn't be likely to experiment with a full-size aluminum wing that might be 100 feet long. It would be much more practical to make a *model* wing 10 inches long, built of wood or cardboard.

Another reason to make a model is to try out an idea. You can experiment with a rough model, exploring the different possibilities. Then, when it is working the way you want, you can go ahead and build a neat, carefully constructed, finished version of your invention.

Making a model may sound like a difficult undertaking. And sometimes it is. If your invention is very intricate, with many complicated parts, a working model may be beyond the skills and tools that you have. In that case, you'll have to settle for a drawing.

But usually you don't need to make a model this fancy or finely detailed.

The model shown on page 38 could be built by anybody. The drawings on page 41 explain it in some detail. This invention is called a *Shoo-fly!* It shoos flies away from a freshly baked pie. One reason we might call this a model rather than a finished invention is that it is built rather crudely. A rough model was needed to see if the idea really worked and to make changes and try possible variations. If you were to manufacture hundreds of thousands of this revolutionary invention to sell all over the world, the actual construction would have to be much more carefully worked out. No doubt, a mass-produced *Shoo-fly!* would be driven by an electric motor.

With most inventions—serious or otherwise—usually a great deal of adjusting, changing, and general fiddling about is required until you get everything the way you want it. You must never give up too soon. Sometimes your original idea just

The only materials used in this invention are a funnel, two tin cans, some plastic strips, a spool, feathers, a cork, a metal rod, and some scraps of wood. The sand in the upper can goes through the funnel and falls onto the plastic fins on the spool. This causes the spool to revolve and also turn the cork to which the feathers are attached. The feathers will shoo away even the most persistent fly. An invention like this is, of course, built just for the fun of it. If you really wanted to keep flies off your pie, you would seal it with plastic wrap or put it in the refrigerator—or eat it up right away!

won't do and you will have to start all over again, trying to work it out in some other shape or form or with other materials —or if worse comes to worse you may find the invention is just plain unworkable and you'll have to move on to some other great idea. (Thomas Edison tried thousands of different materials for the filament of his electric light bulb before he finally found one that worked.)

Of course, not all inventions involve mechanical parts or materials such as wood, metal, or plastic. Some inventions may use fabric or clay or rubber, or electric or chemical materials. If, for example, you invented a pair of garter-suspenders that would hold up your socks and your pants at the same time, your model would probably make use of cloth and elastic and require more sewing with needle and thread than hammering or gluing.

The following chapter explains some of the methods and materials for model building. Of course, if your invention was a new kind of candy that was a combination of sugar, water, and spinach, you couldn't very well make a model, though you could make a sample. Ugh!

Drawings

Sometimes you simply don't have the place to work or the tools and materials to make a model. Or you just don't *want* to make a model. Then drawings will have to do the job. Actually, a serious inventor would make drawings as well as a model, and he or she would use the drawings as a guide for the construction of the model, or even of the full-size invention. An engineer would make very precise drawings that would require exact measurements, mechanical drawing tools, and patience and skill. But for our purposes, simple sketches or diagrams made with pencil or pen will do. The only tools you need are a ruler and perhaps a compass.

No drawing skill is needed if you have a clear idea of just what it is you are trying to draw. Most people are very timid about making any kind of drawing. "I can't draw a straight line," they complain. I always reply, "Neither can I. I use a ruler!"

The two drawings opposite explain the Shoo-fly invention shown on page 38. The first drawing is the preliminary one and it is very rough. Here the inventor was exploring the idea and trying out on paper various ways of getting things to work. The second drawing is done with much more care. It shows in detail just how all the parts are fitted together and what the sizes are. Showing two views of the invention helps to make the workings of it easier to understand. Sometimes a third view, from above, can be further help.

The main thing to remember when doing *your* drawing is that it isn't supposed to be a work of art. It is a record of your idea, and an explanation. It is something to have so that the idea won't be forgotten. It is something to help you explain your idea to other people. Even if a drawing is crude, it will usually explain an idea better than a lot of talk.

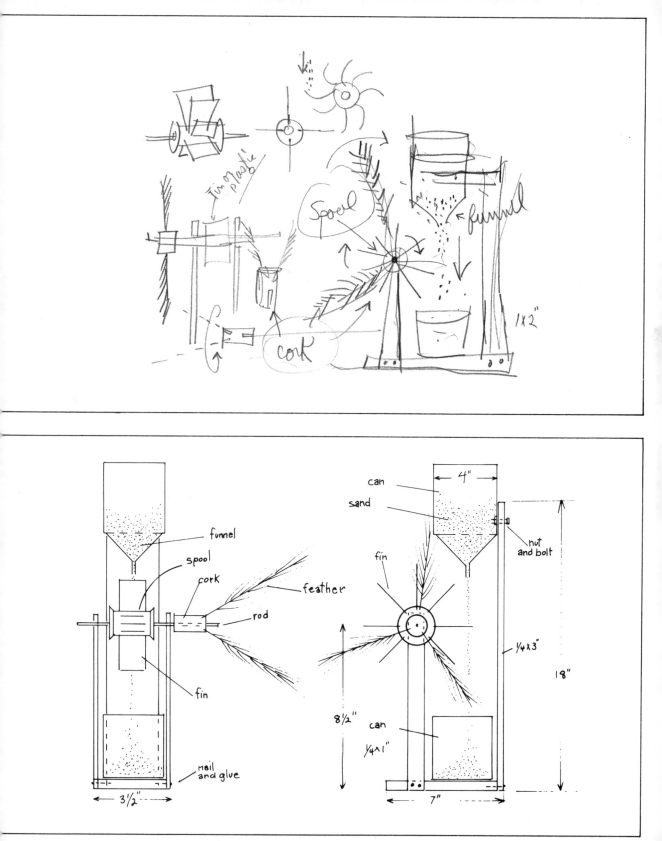

The drawings on these two pages are both by Robert Fulton. They show two different ways of illustrating an idea. The drawing above is really a painting. (Fulton was a professional artist before he was an inventor.) It shows how his submarine would look sailing on top of the water. Then in the lower half of the picture we see what happens when the sails are removed, the mast is lowered, and the boat (or submarine) anchored below the surface of the water.

The other drawing is something quite different. It is an example of a mechanical drawing done with ruler and compass. It explains some of the mechanical details of a different kind of submarine that Fulton was experimenting with. This submarine was designed in 1798 and was called the *Nautilus*. It had no motor. Power was to be provided by two husky men turning cranks connected to the propeller. It is a little uncertain where the air they would need to keep breathing was to come from.

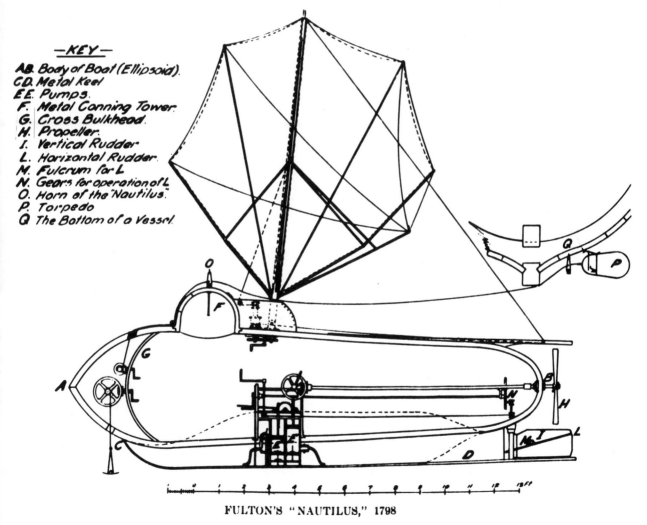

—KEY—

AB. Body of Boat (Ellipsoid).
CD. Metal Keel
EE. Pumps.
F. Metal Conning Tower.
G. Cross Bulkhead.
H. Propeller.
I. Vertical Rudder.
L. Horizontal Rudder.
M. Fulcrum for L
N. Gears for operation of L
O. Horn of the "Nautilus".
P. Torpedo
Q The Bottom of a Vessel.

FULTON'S "NAUTILUS," 1798

43

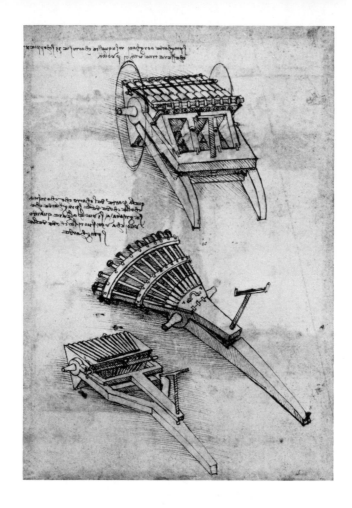

These two drawings are from the sketchbooks of Leonardo da Vinci. Da Vinci was such a fine artist that even when he was simply trying to explain an idea for an invention, the resulting drawings turned out to be works of art—as these drawings certainly are. The notes and comments on the drawings are difficult to read, not only because they are in Italian, but because they are written backward. Da Vinci didn't want uninvited snoopers or unauthorized guests stealing his ideas. There are more da Vinci drawings and models later in the book, and on page 75 there is a photograph of a model of the multiple-barrel cannon shown above.

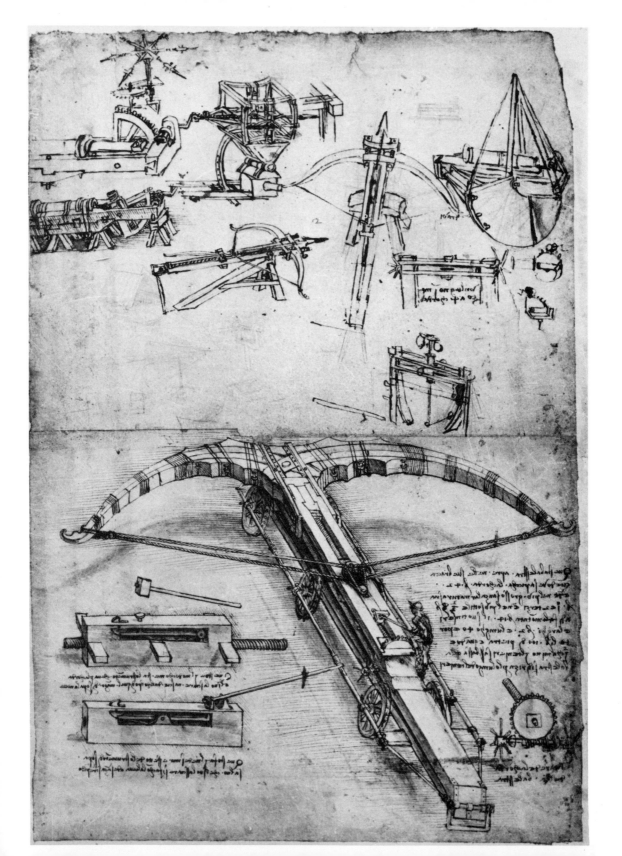

Making It Work
Useful Data
for the Inventor

Professional inventors work in many different fields—electricity, chemistry, botany, optics, aeronautics, hydraulics, nuclear physics, and just about every other area you can think of. But amateur inventors, who are often working for the fun of it, find that they are frequently using commonplace materials such as wood or tin, or small electric motors, pulleys, bits of plastic, and odds and ends found in the house or at the local hardware store. Not many amateurs will have the use of a nuclear reactor, an electron microscope, a turret lathe, a wind tunnel, or any of the fancy and expensive equipment available to the professional inventor or scientist.

The sorts of inventions most amateurs get involved with are of a somewhat mechanical nature, so this chapter focusses on that kind of invention and describes some of the materials you, as an amateur, are most likely to make use of. It shows different ways of attaching parts and getting things to move. It lists a lot of little operations and ideas, and includes hints and suggestions you may be able to use in your own inventions.

Materials

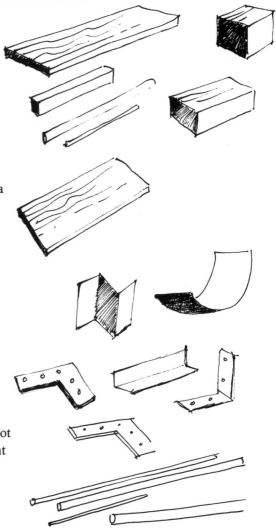

Wood is available in all sizes and thicknesses. Because it is easy to cut, drill, and shape, it is ideal for various purposes.

Plywood is best avoided for small parts. It has a bad habit of splintering when cut and the edges are hard to finish off neatly. It is fine for large-scale construction, however.

Sheet metal is handy where a thin material is wanted. It can be bent, cut with a hacksaw or metal shears, and can be drilled.

Steel angles and strips can be found in any hardware store.

Dowels are wooden rods. They come in three-foot lengths in various diameters. They can be bought in any hardware store or lumberyard. They are useful for such things as axles, supports, and struts and are nice looking. Old broom or mop handles will also be useful on occasion.

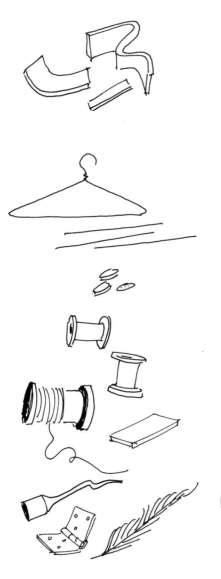

Plastic comes in various types and sizes. Plexiglass can be obtained in different thicknesses. It can be heated in an oven and bent or twisted and will hold its shape when cooled. The thin plastic used for food containers can be cut up into all kinds of shapes.

Cardboard comes in different thicknesses and is especially useful for nonworking models or where strength is not important.

Stiff wire can be obtained by cutting up a wire coat hanger. Paper clips are another possibility.

It is impossible to list all the materials you may need because every invention will have its own requirements. You may find you need some odd material like feathers or an old toothbrush, a scrap of leather, some buttons, or a rubber tire. On occasion, rather unlikely materials will be what you want—clay or straw or wax or sawdust or cloth or . . .

Attaching Parts

Most inventions, especially the more mechanical kind, consist of several parts that have to be attached to one another in some way. Several possibilities are shown here.

Glue will do a good job of attaching two pieces of wood together if the two pieces fit neatly. A white glue such as Elmer's works fine with wood. There are many other special-purpose glues and cements such as epoxy or model-makers glue that are also useful at times. Most glues require that the parts somehow be clamped together until the glue sets. Read the directions on the container before using.

Glued joints can often be made a lot stronger by fastening a small wood block in the corner for reinforcement.

Nuts and bolts are neat and strong and can be used to join all kinds of materials.

Screws are very often useful.

Nails come to mind first when you think of joining two or more pieces of wood. But you must use the right size nail—too large and the wood will split, too small and the nail won't hold. Avoid nailing close to the edge of your wood or you'll get splits.

Lacing or wrapping will sometimes suit a particular situation.

Dowels will hold two pieces of wood together securely. Drill holes of the appropriate size. Coat the dowel with glue and hammer into place.

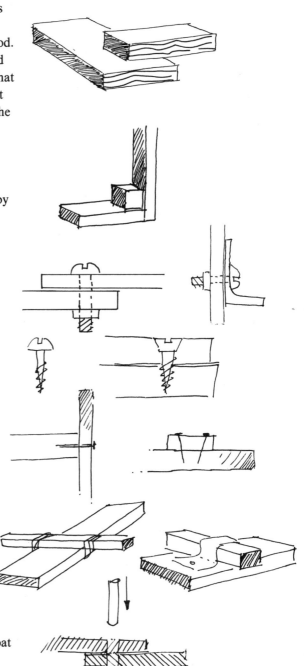

Some Basic Sources of Power

Many inventions have moving parts and require some sort of power. A few of the possibilities are shown here.

Some free sources of power are wind, flowing water, the sun, and the movement of the tides. With energy conservation an important concern today, these natural power sources are receiving a lot of attention.

The hand crank is a simple and reliable way to get things to move. If a string is attached to the center of the shaft, weights can be easily raised or lowered. Another possibility is to connect gears to the protruding end of the shaft to turn all kinds of mechanisms.

Gravity is something we take for granted, but it is also a source of power. In this case the basket will be raised when the weight falls off the edge of the table.

It is gravity that is making the sand fall down onto the rotating paddle wheel. This is how the Shoo-fly invention on page 38 is powered.

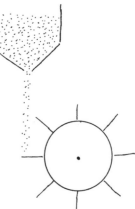

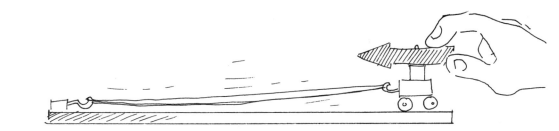

A rubber band is one of the amateur inventor's best friends. It can be made to do all sorts of things.

A rubber band, like a spring, is not really a source of power. It is a way to store power. The power comes from your hand when you stretch the rubber band, or twist it, or extend or compress a spring.

Free sources of power:
flowing water, the wind, and the sun.

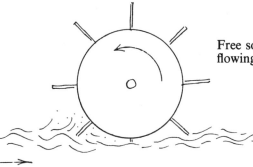

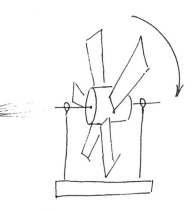

Using Electricity

Electricity in one form or another is a part of many different types of inventions. It can be used to produce light, heat, and various kinds of motion.

Electric motors are a useful, easy-to-find source of power. They are simple to remove from old, broken washing machines, vacuum cleaners, fans, and other household appliances. These motors usually work on 110 volts.

This is a common type of motor, one that you might find in certain kinds of shop equipment or in home appliances. Often you can find a perfectly good motor in the innards of a discarded washing or drying machine or a similar piece of household equipment. Motors like this, which operate on 110 volts, have a lot more power than you are likely to need.

Motors like these, which can be found inside most electric clocks, also run on 110 volts. Even if the clock doesn't work and seems a hopeless wreck, you will usually find that the motor, once removed from the wreckage, will perform perfectly. The little stubby gear that sticks up out of the casing is geared down to turn very slowly. Be sure to read the cautionary note about the dangers involved in using such motors.

Small motors that work on 1½, 3, 6, or 12 volts can be bought in electrical supply stores or hobby shops. These work on batteries.

These little motors are about an inch and a half long. This particular kind comes with a little gear already attached. They will run jauntily on a 1½-volt battery. However they will have quite a bit more power with 3 volts to work on.

DANGER! The kind of electricity that is used to work household lights and appliances is 110 volts, and if it is not handled with some know-how it can produce a dangerous, painful shock. If you have had no experience with electricity, get a book and read up on it, or get somebody to show you what it's all about.

If you are inexperienced with electricity, avoid 110 volts and work with small motors that operate on 1½, 3, 6, or 12 volts. This kind of electricity comes from batteries and is perfectly safe. The voltage is too low to shock you or injure you in any way.

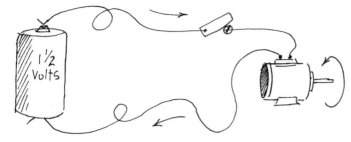

In order to turn off any electric device without disconnecting a wire, you need a way to interrupt the complete circuit. A switch of some sort will do this.

A simple switch can be made from a piece of tin and two screws. The tin can be swung back and forth to make or break contact.

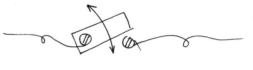

If you want to connect wires to a small battery, you can put together the holder shown here. All you need are two pieces of tin, some tape, and a rubber band.

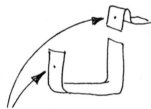

Punch holes in toward where the battery will be so that the jagged edges of the holes make firm contact with the battery terminals. Punch two more holes so that you can connect the wires. All wire used in electrical devices must be copper and insulated. Insulation is the wrapping or plastic coating that covers the bare metal.

Wrap this part with tape.

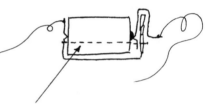

A rubber band or two around the holder will keep the contacts tight against the battery terminals.

Inventors have spent a lot of time devising various kinds of burglar alarms. By working out a system of electrical contacts, it is possible to set off buzzers or bells or lights when a door is opened or a window tampered with.

An electromagnet can be made from a large nail or bolt wrapped with wire and then connected to a battery.

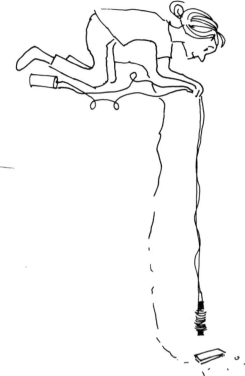

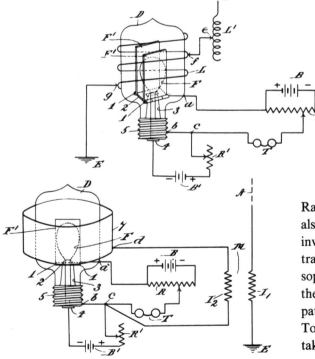

If you know something about electricity, you can use a variety of more complicated electric parts in your inventions—relays, transformers, photo-cells, special switches, and so on.

Radio and electronic inventions are also possibilities for the amateur inventor if he or she has had some training and experience in this rather sophisticated field. The drawings on the left are from Lee De Forest's patent application for a radio tube. Today, small size transistors have taken the place of most radio tubes.

Mechanical Motion

The drawings here illustrate a few of the not-too-complicated ways you can get things to move.

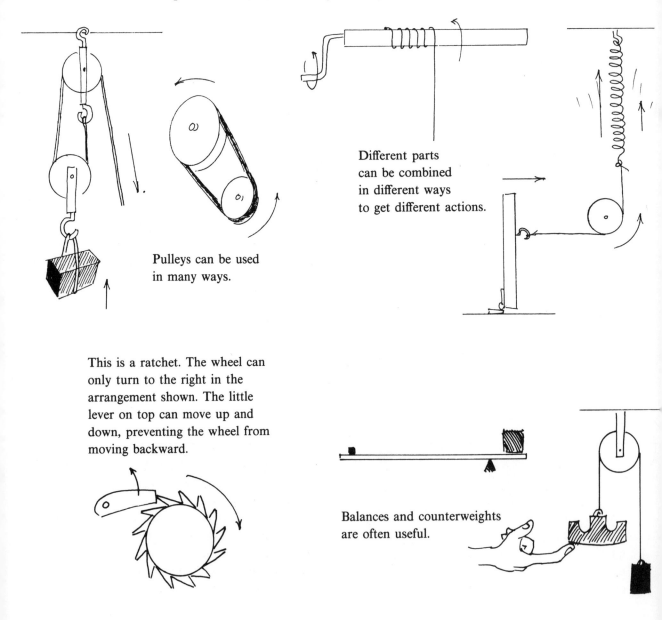

Pulleys can be used in many ways.

Different parts can be combined in different ways to get different actions.

This is a ratchet. The wheel can only turn to the right in the arrangement shown. The little lever on top can move up and down, preventing the wheel from moving backward.

Balances and counterweights are often useful.

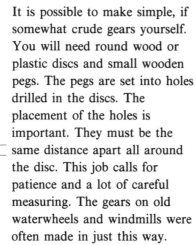

It is possible to make simple, if somewhat crude gears yourself. You will need round wood or plastic discs and small wooden pegs. The pegs are set into holes drilled in the discs. The placement of the holes is important. They must be the same distance apart all around the disc. This job calls for patience and a lot of careful measuring. The gears on old waterwheels and windmills were often made in just this way.

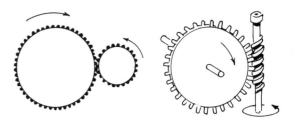

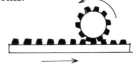

Gears come in all sizes, shapes, and forms.

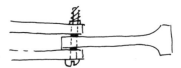

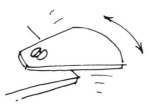

Simple pivots can be made using nuts and bolts or wood screws.

This is a crank. It changes a rotating movement to a back and forth movement or vice versa. This action is used in the steam engine and in the gasoline engine.

Here is a cam. This one is like a wheel with an off-center point of rotation. As the cam rotates, the beam moves up and down.

You can find more detailed information about mechanical motion in encyclopedias and other reference books.

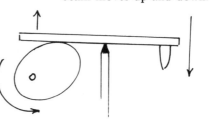

Some Ideas for Inventors

If you don't already have a *great idea* that is going to make the world sit up and take notice, here are a number of suggestions that may get you started on an invention of your own.

There are no step-by-step instructions. If there were, the invention would be already invented! The purpose of this chapter is simply to suggest possibilities, areas for investigation, places in the home, garden, workshop, and kitchen where you might find a need for a practical and useful invention.

Some inventions may require complicated parts or special equipment. That sort of invention is best avoided, especially if you are a beginner. But if you do find yourself in the middle of a project that is a little more than you can handle, see if you can get someone who knows something about your problem to help you out. Or get some books and read up on the subject in question.

These suggestions assume that you have just the usual household odds and ends and simple tools to work with, and no particular skills or training. If you have experience in specialized fields, you can develop much more complicated inventions than the sort mentioned here.

Bear in mind that most inventions are improvements on or changes in devices that already exist. There are not too many inventions that are completely new and revolutionary.

A pen and pencil holder

A new kind of lamp for reading in bed

A storage box with a secret compartment

A new kind of sailboat or land sailer

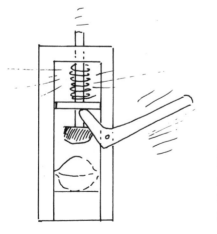

A better design for a nutcracker is a challenge that has intrigued inventors through the ages. Perhaps you can come up with a bright new idea for the ultimate nutcracker . . . the simple (or complicated or silly) gadget that the world has been waiting for!

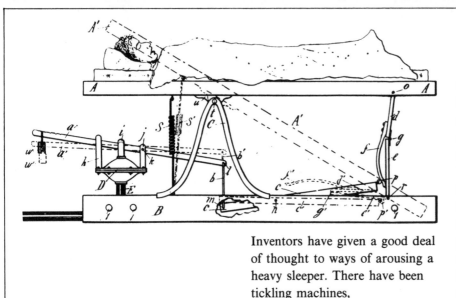

water-dumping apparatuses, blanket pulling gadgets, and so on. But perhaps the strangest and most violent invention is the one shown here, patented in 1900. It is triggered by a temperature-sensing device. In the early morning, when the temperature falls to a certain point, a series of levers and catches release the foot of the bed and the sleeper is—*clunk*—dumped out!

Inventors have given a good deal of thought to ways of arousing a heavy sleeper. There have been tickling machines,

A closet organizer—a tie rack, a shoe holder, etc.

A magazine rack—one that rotates or folds away

Optical devices using lenses, mirrors, and prisms

Games using springs or ball bearings, marbles, cards, dice, or spinners

A music stand with a light

Photo darkroom gadgets

There are many toy possibilities for the inventor—toys that hang, pull along, are motorized, or that can be taken apart and reassembled.

Games for two players using balls, nets, racquets, etc.

Ways to get waked up in the morning

Submarines, land and moon rovers, ocean-bottom crawlers

Remote control devices for camera, TV, or tape recorder

Windmills and waterwheels

A new kind of wood-burning stove

Automatic page turner that lets you eat and read at the same time

Here is a very "practical" kind of fly killer. The cannon shoots a ball of honey that the fly likes so much it will eat itself to death.

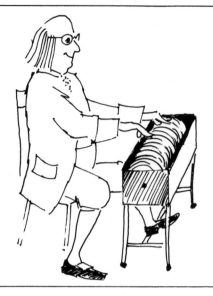

Benjamin Franklin liked the sound that is produced when you wet a finger and run it around the edge of a glass. He arranged thirty-seven glass hemispheres of varying sizes and thicknesses and mounted them on a horizontal rod that could be turned by a foot treadle. By wetting the glass with a sponge and pressing the fingers against the rims as they turned, a melody could be played.

A moving scarecrow for the garden

A new kind of kite

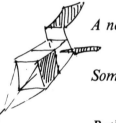

Something for the family car

Bathtub devices—to hold books, to scrub your back, to hold the soap and shampoo

A new kind of wallet or purse

Ways to collect energy from the sun

Every kitchen has storage problems. Perhaps you can design a new kind of holder for silverware or dishes or pots and pans.

A vest to hold tools or camera equipment

This is a more complex invention for killing flies. The fellow sitting on the stool is eating a watermelon and spitting out the pits with great force. The gadget on his head is a sighting mechanism so that the operator can take aim at the fly and point the watermelon eater in the right direction. (This invention has never been patented.)

Weather vanes and wind-speed indicators

A way to water plants when you go on vacation

A desk-top savings bank with a secret way to open it in times of financial emergencies

An inventor by the name of Otto Lilienthal was experimenting in 1894 with something that looks very much like the hang gliders that are so popular today.

This invention might be entitled "There's Nothing New under the Sun." The engraving shows a printing press that was operated by solar energy—a source of energy that is much thought about these days. The large parabolic mirror concentrated the sun's heat on the small boiler mounted in the center of the reflector. The heat boils the water, making steam that operates the steam engine shown in the left foreground. And this, in turn, powers the printing press on the right. It is said that this apparatus really was set up in 1882 and actually worked for several hours.

Bird feeders

Bicycle improvements, such as a speedometer, mileage indicator, tow cart, or book rack

A display system for stamps or coins or butterflies or whatever

Model airplanes, gliders, helicopters, and hot air balloons

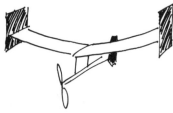

Pipe and tobacco holder

Stationery holder and stamp dispenser with paper clip storage

(Most successful inventions grow out of personal knowledge and experience. They are based on something you know all about!)

Ways to send messages or signals

Musical instruments using rods, rubber bands, glass, metal strips, gongs, etc.

A new kind of time-keeping mechanism

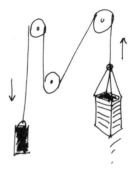

A color slide viewer

Weighing and measuring devices

Clothing improvements—special pockets and holders, hats, a scarf with pockets, earmuffs with nose warmer

Robots

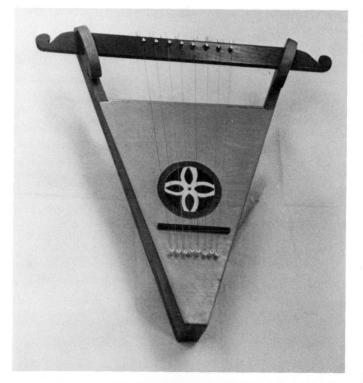

This musical instrument—a kind of simple harp—was invented and constructed by a young man who had nothing to work with other than a board, a piece of plywood, some miscellaneous odds and ends, and a few hand tools.

Patents

A patent is protection for an invention. It is issued to the inventor by the federal government Patent Office. The inventor submits his or her idea, clearly explained with drawings and in a written statement. If the Patent Office decides the idea is genuinely new and practical, it will grant a patent to the inventor.

A patent says in effect that such-and-such an idea has been produced by the inventor. It is that person's idea alone, his or her property, and nobody can use this idea without the permission of the inventor. The inventor is free to sell the idea, or to

A number of inventors give a great deal of thought, time, and energy to devices that seem worthwhile, look nice, and yet never really work in any useful sort of way. The wind-engine shown here is a case in point. It is really a kind of windmill turned on its side. The vertical shaft, which the sails cause to turn, is geared to a pair of wheels that move the whole awkward thing along the ground. As the wind-engine moves, a plow at the rear turns over the soil . . . or so Mr. J. Cook hoped. The trouble with this invention, patented in 1878, is that not much plowing would get done unless it was a windy day . . . if then!

J. COOK.
Wind-Engine.

No. 209,862. Patented Nov. 12, 1878.

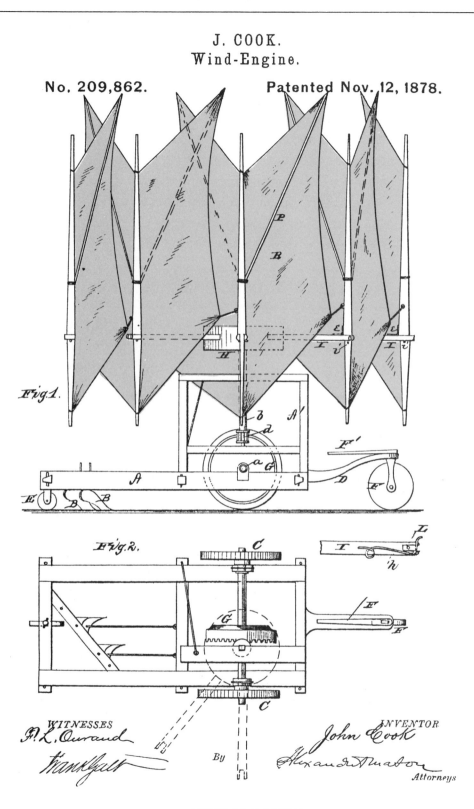

Fig.1.

Fig.2.

WITNESSES
F. L. Ourand
Frank Galt

By

INVENTOR
John Cook

Alexander Mason
Attorneys

N. PETERS, PHOTO-LITHOGRAPHER, WASHINGTON, D C.

allow someone to manufacture the invention for a fee or for a royalty payment. Nobody can simply take another person's patented idea and use it without authorization. Those who do will find themselves in all kinds of legal trouble. However, a patent doesn't protect an invention forever. It is only good for seventeen years. After that anybody can use the idea.

The first United States patent was granted in 1790. In Europe the idea of protecting the inventor dates back to well before that time.

For many years the United States Patent Office required that an inventor submit a model as well as drawings for the invention he or she wanted to patent. This requirement resulted in an enormous accumulation of models of all kinds—including some very fancy, and sometimes rather ridiculous, constructions. At one time hundreds of thousands of models filled every available nook and cranny of the Patent Office. Finally, in 1870, actual models were banned.

Over the years there were several disastrous fires in the Patent Office buildings, and many of the most interesting models were destroyed. However, a great many still remained, gathering dust in government attics and warehouses. The storage space was needed, so the models were eventually sold off. Even today, though, a number of these old models still exist, owned by individuals and stored in unopened cases in barns and sheds, waiting till time, money, and space is available for their unpacking.

Some of the most famous models are owned by the Smithsonian Institute in Washington, D. C., and can be seen there. One model was made by none other than Abraham Lincoln. He patented his invention in 1849. It was described as a New and Improved Manner of Buoying Vessels over Shoals.

This is one of the old Patent Office models. It was recently pulled out of the case in which it had been stored for many years. Some old models have lost their identifying tags and nobody is quite sure just what the invention is all about. But with many of them the workmanship is so skilled and the materials—fine woods, polished steel and brass—so handsome that the models are valued as simply beautiful, if somewhat mysterious objects. Perhaps you can figure out what this invention was supposed to do.

The business of applying for a patent is neither simple nor inexpensive. It is not an undertaking to embark upon lightly. Briefly, this is the way it is done: A search is made in the records of the Patent Office to see if there is an invention like yours already patented. If there is, you don't get a patent. The next step is the filing of the formal patent application, which must include an accurate and complete description of the invention.

Both steps are much more complicated than they sound, and they require the services of experts who are familiar with the many requirements of the Patent Office. If you think you have hit on something unique as well as practical, you should send for the government pamphlet mentioned at the back of this book. It explains in detail the entire process of applying for a

Here is the drawing for the improved "Burial Case." A string attached to a bell was placed in the body's hand. He could ring for help if it turned out that he wasn't really dead. (Hopefully someone would be within earshot!) There was also a spring-operated lid and a ladder leading through an air shaft to above ground. If there was no action after a period of time, the bell, ladder, and air shaft could be removed and the matter considered finished.

patent, and has a section of answers to questions most often asked about patents.

There are certain organizations that advertise widely, offering to help inventors patent and market their ideas. Some of these advertisers are more interested in making money from the innocent inventor than in helping the inventor make a success of his or her idea. They should be approached with a great deal of caution and suspicion.

Often it is not worth the trouble and expense to get a patent on your invention. The services of a patent attorney and all the fees required will run to many hundreds of dollars. Unless an invention is practical and is likely to earn a profit or be of some real use, there is no point in getting a patent. A patent is of no value in itself. Why go to the trouble of patenting an idea if nobody wants it?

Considering the enormous number of patents that the Patent Office has granted over the years, it should be no surprise that quite a few have been issued for bizarre, impractical, or downright weird inventions. A few of these inventions are shown here. The "improved" safety coffin was patented at a time when many people had a fear of being buried prematurely. In 1868, when this patent was granted, medical science was evidently not quite sure how to determine if a person was honestly and truly dead! The bereaved family, the inventor assumed, wouldn't want to take any chances.

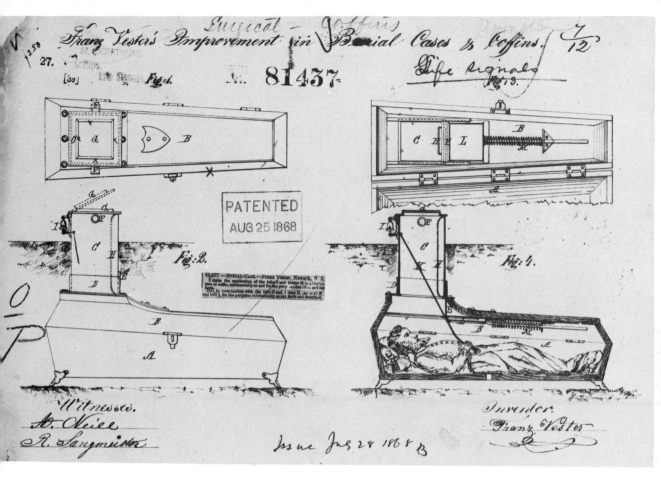

The steam-operated tricycle shown in this old engraving is not as impractical as it may at first appear. There are quite a few experimental cars and motorcycles driving around today that are propelled by steam engines.

Some Famous Inventors and Their Inventions

Leonardo da Vinci

Leonardo da Vinci is known primarily as an artist. But like many artists, he was fascinated by all kinds of mechanical devices. He was born in 1452 and lived until 1519, and during that time he developed an enormous number of ideas, many of them way ahead of their time. He kept a series of notebooks describing his thoughts and discoveries. The illustration opposite is a page from one of these books. His handwriting looks odd because he wrote backwards in order to confuse the uninvited viewer.

His notebooks contain anatomical drawings as well as de-

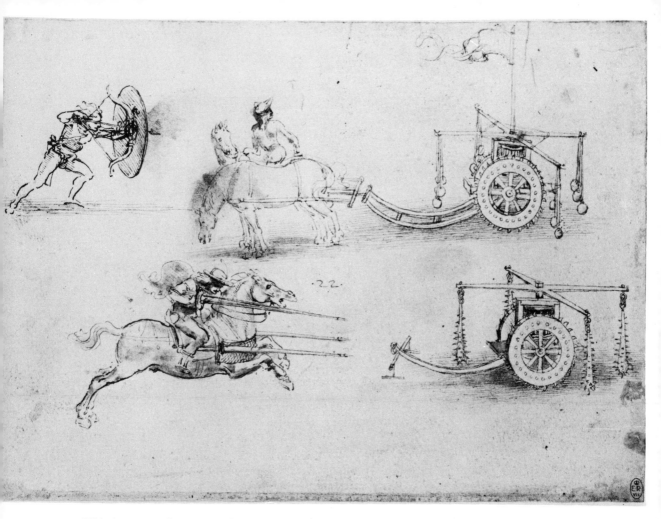

This is a page from one of Leonardo da Vinci's sketchbooks. It shows three inventions. On the upper left is a design for a combination bow and arrow and shield. Although the drawing doesn't seem to show it, we can assume there is a slot or peephole in the shield so that the archer can see what he is shooting at. On the lower left is a plan for mounting two spears on the saddle of a horse. An array of horses with spears like this charging at the enemy would be likely to make even the bravest person turn and run. The other two drawings show a more complicated and quite mean-looking mechanism. Iron balls or fearsome clubs are attached to four arms. The wheels are geared to a central shaft, and as the carriage was pulled along and the wheels turned, the balls or clubs would swing out from the ends of the rotating arms. If you got in the way, that would be your last look at a da Vinci invention!

scriptions of gears and levers, flying machines, clock mechanisms, and weapons—ambitious plans of all sorts. Some of his ideas were very advanced. For example, practical flying machines were not invented until hundreds of years later.

This da Vinci invention is for roasting a pig. A fan placed near the top of the chimney is turned by the rising, heated air from the fire. The fan is connected through a series of gears to the spit on which the pig is impaled. The pig will revolve over the flames and get cooked on all sides. This cutaway model, like the models on the facing page, was not built by da Vinci but was constructed from drawings in his sketchbooks.

Leonardo was fascinated with the form of the spiral, and he uses it in this design for a helicopter, which is a form of aerial screw. He wrote of this invention, "If this instrument made with a screw be well made—that is to say, made with linen of which the pores are stopped up with starch—and be turned swiftly, the said screw will make its spiral in the air and it will rise up high." Below is a triple-tier set of cannons. There are eleven barrels in each tier. While one set of barrels is fired, another tier is loaded and the third cools. This design and other weapons da Vinci devised show him constantly attempting to achieve more efficient firepower.

Benjamin Franklin

Benjamin Franklin was many things besides an inventor. He was a diplomat, a statesman of great importance in the early years of this country, a writer, a man of business, a printer, and a publisher. He invented the Franklin stove, a type of wood-burning stove still in use today. He also invented bifocal glasses when he was eighty-three years old and had trouble seeing. His most important scientific experiments, however, had to do with electricity.

He is, of course, well known for flying a kite up into a thunderstorm and observing the electricity that sparked off a key tied to the string. This is a dangerous experiment, and Franklin was lucky to have survived it. Other people trying the same thing have been killed by severe electric shocks.

Franklin refused to patent any of his inventions. He considered them his contribution to society.

Robert Fulton

When he was twenty-eight years old, Robert Fulton gave up a career as an artist and turned his full attention to science and engineering. He produced many inventions, including the submarines illustrated earlier in the book and on pages 78 and 79. His most famous invention, however, was the steamboat *Clermont,* shown below.

Like many inventors, Fulton combined already existing parts in a new way. The steam engine of the *Clermont* was built in a more or less conventional way. And the boat in which the engine was installed was nothing out of the ordinary. What Fulton did for the first time was combine a hull, engine, and

system of paddle wheels into one practical and commercially profitable boat that could carry passengers up and down the Hudson River. The first commercial voyage of the *Clermont* was in 1807.

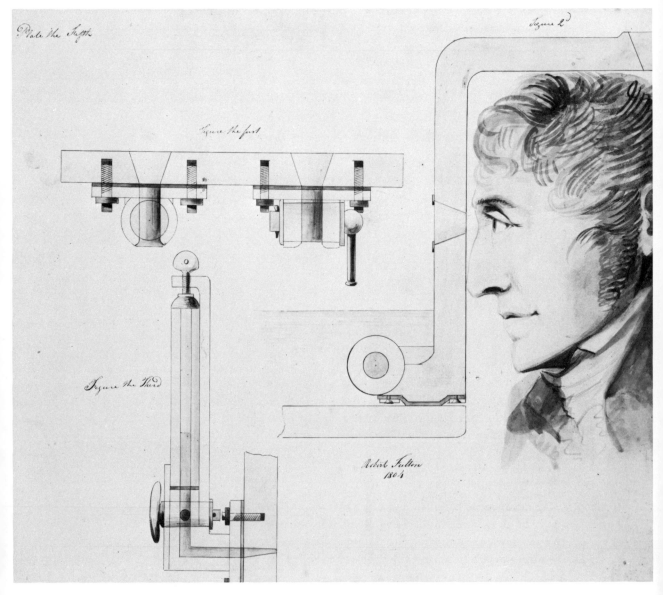

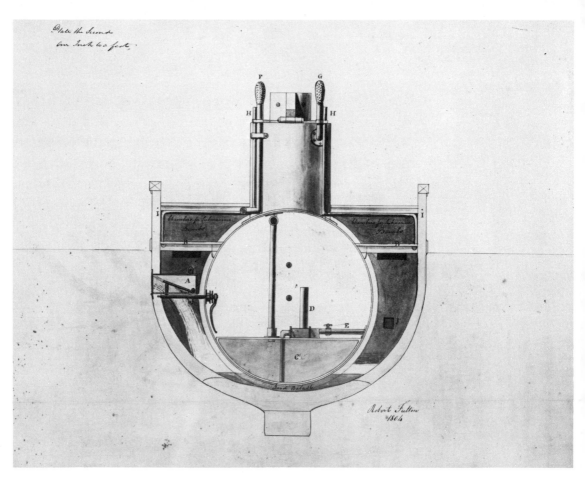

This cross-sectional drawing of the submarine shows how Fulton
intended to open a valve to permit water to enter between the inner and
outer hull. The mechanism in the center is, no doubt, a pump that
would expel the water when it came time to surface. Fulton actually did
build a working submarine that was financed by none other than the
Emperor Napoleon. It was propelled by a system of hand cranks and in
1800 was submerged for forty-five minutes in the river Seine in Paris.
Napoleon wanted to use Fulton's invention against the British. But the
vessel was not really seaworthy. Two other of Fulton's plans for
submarines are shown on pages 42 and 43.

In this drawing made over a hundred and fifty years ago, Fulton shows
how he plans to fit an eyepiece in the turret of his submarine. He
obviously couldn't resist the temptation to do a painterly portrait at the
same time he was doing the mechanically precise drawing of the
eyepiece.

George Stephenson

There were many inventors who had a hand in the development of the railways, but George Stephenson, born in England in 1781, was probably the most important. Stephenson and his son, Robert (1803–1859), managed to efficiently connect the steam engine, which had already been invented, to a set of wheels that could run along steel tracks. (This is all a steam locomotive is.) George Stephenson also worked out many of the engineering problems involved in getting train tracks to run over bridges and through varied terrains.

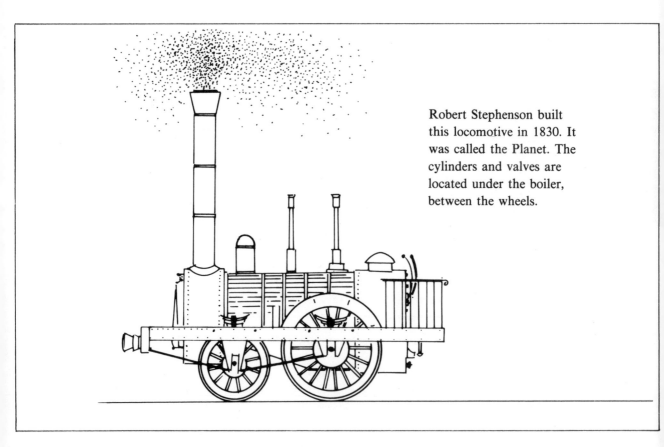

Robert Stephenson built this locomotive in 1830. It was called the Planet. The cylinders and valves are located under the boiler, between the wheels.

Over the last 150 years locomotives like the Planet have gradually been improved in size and power. The plantation locomotive is about a halfway step toward the massive engine shown below.

This powerful locomotive was about the end of the line for this kind of steam power. Today most locomotives are diesel-powered and aren't nearly as much fun to watch in action.

Eli Whitney

Eli Whitney is best known for his invention of the cotton gin. Before the machine was invented, the production of cotton was a tedious and expensive operation because the cotton had to be separated by hand from the seeds of the plant. Whitney's gin did this job automatically, thus making cotton cheap to buy and more readily available.

But just as important as the cotton gin were Whitney's ideas about mass production and the interchangeability of parts. In 1798 he was given a contract by the government to manufacture a large quantity of small arms. Up until that time, rifles and handguns had been made one at a time by single craftsmen. A broken part could not easily be replaced—it had to be made by hand and carefully fitted to the already existing parts in the gun. This was slow, skilled work. Whitney's idea was to make standardized parts for his guns, using precise manufacturing methods. This meant that if the trigger of a gun broke, it could easily be replaced with another trigger exactly like it.

This method of mass production is now commonly used in the production of everything from automobiles and television receivers to shoelaces.

Rube Goldberg

Rube Goldberg was not really an inventor. He was a cartoonist and illustrator. For many years he wrote and illustrated a cartoon series about the absentminded Professor Butts, who kept coming up with the most preposterous inventions. The cartoons appeared in newspapers all over the country. They were so popular and so well known that the phrase "Rube Goldberg" became a part of the American vocabulary. "Rube Goldberg" has come to mean any overly complicated, ridiculous device.

If you were to put together an invention with a great many peculiar, impractical parts that did something silly in a silly way, someone would be sure to look at your idea and say, "Wow, that looks like a Rube Goldberg!"

Two typical Rube Goldberg cartoons explaining inventions by Professor Butts are shown on the next two pages.

PROFESSOR BUTTS GETS CAUGHT IN A
REVOLVING DOOR AND BECOMES DIZZY
ENOUGH TO DOPE OUT AN IDEA TO KEEP
YOU FROM FORGETTING TO MAIL YOUR
WIFE'S LETTER.
AS YOU WALK PAST COBBLER SHOP, HOOK(A)
STRIKES SUSPENDED BOOT(B)CAUSING IT TO
KICK FOOTBALL(C)THROUGH GOAL POSTS(D).
FOOTBALL DROPS INTO BASKET(E)AND STRING
(F)TILTS SPRINKLING CAN(G)CAUSING WATER
TO SOAK COAT TAILS(H).AS COAT SHRINKS
CORD(I)OPENS DOOR(J)OF CAGE ALLOWING
BIRD(K)TO WALK OUT ON PERCH(L)AND GRABS
WORM(M)WHICH IS ATTACHED TO STRING(N).
THIS PULLS DOWN WINDOW SHADE(O)ON
WHICH IS WRITTEN,"YOU SAP, MAIL
THAT LETTER". A SIMPLE WAY TO
AVOID ALL THIS TROUBLE IS TO MARRY
A WIFE WHO CAN'T WRITE.

Rube Goldberg explains here
how his cartoon character,
Professor Butts, invents an
apparatus to remind the
absentminded to mail a letter.

A SAFE FALLS ON THE HEAD OF PROFESSOR BUTTS AND KNOCKS OUT AN IDEA FOR HIS LATEST SIMPLE FLY SWATTER.

CARBOLIC ACID (A) DRIPS ON STRING (B) CAUSING IT TO BREAK AND RELEASE ELASTIC OF BEAN SHOOTER (C) WHICH PROJECTS BALL (D) INTO BUNCH OF GARLIC (E) CAUSING IT TO FALL INTO SYRUP CAN (F) AND SPLASH SYRUP VIOLENTLY AGAINST SIDE WALL. FLY (G) BUZZES WITH GLEE AND GOES FOR SYRUP, HIS FAVORITE DISH. BUTLER-DOG (H) MISTAKES HUM OF FLY'S WINGS FOR DOOR BUZZER AND RUNS TO MEET VISITOR, PULLING ROPE (I) WHICH TURNS STOP-GO SIGNAL (J) AND CAUSES BASEBALL BAT (K) TO SOCK FLY WHO FALLS TO FLOOR UNCONSCIOUS.

AS FLY DROPS TO FLOOR PET TROUT (L) JUMPS FOR HIM, MISSES, AND LANDS IN NET (M). WEIGHT OF FISH FORCES SHOE (N) DOWN ON FALLEN FLY AND PUTS HIM OUT OF THE RUNNING FOR ALL TIME.

IF THE FISH CATCHES THE FLY, THE SHOE CAN BE USED FOR CRACKING NUTS.

Fly swatters are always an interesting challenge for the inventor. The "simple" fly swatter shown here is particularly ingenious.

There are, of course, many other important inventors. A few that you might want to find out more about are:

MICHAEL FARADAY (1791–1867) carried on important experiments with electric current and magnetism.

SAMUEL F. B. MORSE (1791–1872), an artist turned inventor, perfected the telegraph.

W. H. FOX TALBOT (1800–1877) developed some of the basic photographic methods used today.

THOMAS ALVA EDISON (1847–1931), probably America's most famous inventor, devised the electric light, the phonograph, and a number of other things.

HENRY FORD (1863–1947) built the first mass-produced, gasoline-powered automobile.

WILBUR (1867–1912) and ORVILLE (1871–1948) WRIGHT invented the world's first practical powered aircraft.

LOUIS BLÉRIOT (1872–1936) developed early monoplane designs, and in 1909 made the first airborne crossing of the English Channel.

ALBERT EINSTEIN (1879–1955), a theoretical scientist more than a practical inventor, propounded the theory of relativity.

The World's Most Unfamous Invention
and How It Came to Be

The invention illustrated opposite is called a Beckoning Machine. It is my favorite invention . . . mostly because I invented it! It is absolutely useless. It is not the sort of thing a beginning inventor would be likely to get involved with, but it is described here so you can see how an invention develops and perhaps get an idea of the challenge, problem-solving process, and just plain fun of putting your own thing together.

This invention did not start out as a planned, clearly thought-out project. Rather, it grew little by little, with several false starts. It began with the building of a small working steam engine. This was made from a kit of rough parts, which had to

This is how it all started. This is the small steam engine that was assembled from a kit, and which was the beginning of the Beckoning Machine.

be machined and assembled. The engine was built for no other reason than that I happen to love steam engines.

When the engine was finished, the logical thing was to find some use for it. After considerable brainstorming and consideration of alternatives, I decided that I would build a model steam-operated cable car.

A small electric motor that ran on batteries would have been a much more practical source of power. But I had already built the steam engine, steam engines are much more attractive than electric motors—and besides, I didn't really care about being practical.

The cable car was intended to travel along a steel cable that would stretch from the corner of my house to a tree some distance away, and then come back again.

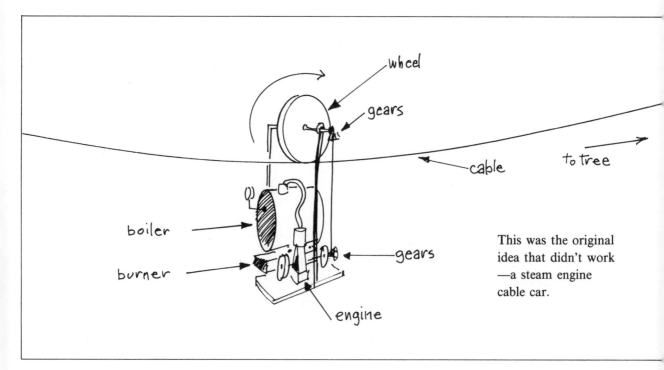

wheel

gears

cable

to tree

boiler

burner

gears

engine

This was the original idea that didn't work —a steam engine cable car.

I had a box of old gears that I had accumulated over the years. (One must never throw *anything* away if one wants to be an inventor!) I figured out a way of getting the steam engine and cable car to connect, through gears, to a large wooden wheel. The wheel had a groove in it, and would roll along the steel cable. (I never did get around to figuring out how I would make the cable car change direction in order to make the return trip.)

However, my great invention didn't work. In fact, it was a terrible failure. The finished cable car was quite heavy. I needed a boiler to produce steam for the engine, and it and all the other parts and gears added up to quite a weight. I found that the engine had enough power to move the car partway along the cable. But the cable sagged in the middle. It was impossible to keep it absolutely straight and horizontal, even when a lot of tension was applied to it. When the cable car got to the middle, "bottom-of-the-hill" section, and then had to go uphill to the far end, it stalled. There just wasn't enough power to move it up the slope. I suppose I could have corrected this by building a straight, stiff, steel rail or track of some sort, but this seemed too elaborate and permanent an installation. The idea of the cable, which I could hook up and take down whenever I wanted, was what I liked.

So there I was, left with a rather complicated mechanism that couldn't do much of anything except turn that big wooden wheel. But I certainly wasn't going to throw away all this time, effort, and thought. Now, what could I use that turning wheel for, or what could I connect it to that would serve some purpose?

If you were presented with this problem, you would certainly come up with an idea entirely different from mine. I worried over this matter for many days. I considered all kinds of pos-

Here is a close-up view of the hand and the finger that beckons.

sibilities, and then somehow thought of a large hand with a finger that would beckon slowly.

A hand carved out of wood wasn't a terribly difficult thing to make. And with a good deal of experimenting and fussing

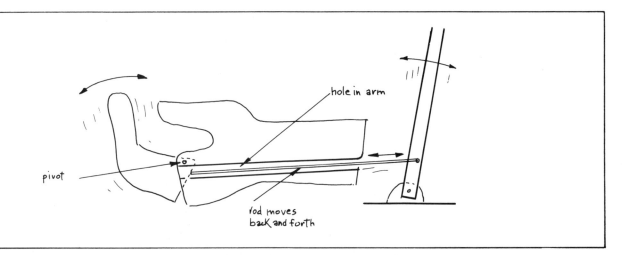

The motion of the beckoning finger is shown in this drawing. The forefinger is held in place by a small rod or pivot, which acts like a hinge. As the long steel rod inside the arm moves back and forth, it causes the finger to move up and down.

about, I managed to work out a way of getting the forefinger to pivot up and down. A little more experimenting and I managed to work out a way of connecting the turning wheel to a lever, which is in turn connected to a rod that I fitted inside the hand, which wiggled the finger.

The rather involved trestle structure that supports the hand, engine, boiler, and other miscellaneous parts serves no special purpose, but I had a lot of thin oak strips handy, and I liked the way the trestle looked.

Now, when I want to entertain myself or visitors and friends, I fire up the boiler, open the valve, and the engine chugs away at a great rate, throwing out clouds of steam, spitting hot oil and spraying everything in sight. The gears turn, the big wheel revolves, the shaft slides in and out, and the forefinger ever so slowly moves up and down.

Sometimes people ask me what I am going to do with this

thing. They don't understand that the fun was in building the machine and getting it to work and look good. But rather than explain all this, I may tell them this is an experimental model for a small, compact version that can be used for scratching an itchy ear, or beckoning a waiter in a restaurant, or scraping dried grease off a frying pan. (For that last operation I suppose I would have to add a sharp fingernail!)

This is a view of the Beckoning Machine from the other side.

Here is a detailed view of the Beckoning Machine. The large box at the rear is the enclosure for the boiler. The round gauge shows what the steam pressure is. When the pressure gets up to around twenty pounds, you can open the main steam valve and start the engine running. The pipe coming out of the boiler box carries the steam to the engine. The black box on the right is a tank to hold water, and the little gadget just in front of it is a hand-operated pump. As the water boils away, more can be pumped from the tank into the boiler. The other small black box just under and to the left of the boiler enclosure holds alcohol, which goes into a burner beneath the boiler.

Reference Material

Every inventor should have a copy of the catalog published by the Edmund Scientific Company. It is free. It is crammed with descriptions of all sorts of kits and gadgets and equipment—gears, lenses, solar cells, motors, telescopes, electrical apparatus, and much more. Just write for a copy to: Edmund Scientific Company, Barrington, New Jersey 08007.

An Information Aid for Inventors. This little pamphlet is a step-by-step guide to getting a patent and marketing an invention. It costs $1.30 and can be ordered from the Superintendent of Documents, U.S. Government Printing Office, Washington, D.C. 20402.

The Way Things Work, published by Simon and Shuster, is an illustrated encyclopedia of technology. It is at times quite complex, but it does describe a great variety of machines and technical operations, from lasers to diesel engines. There is a simplified edition that is shorter and easier to read than the two-volume book.

The Smithsonian Book of Invention, published by the Smithsonian Institute, is a condensed history of invention with many illustrations and photographs of material in the collection of that splendid museum. A visit to the National Museum of History and Technology (which is a division of the Smithsonian Institute in Washington, D.C.) is an experience that nobody interested in inventing should miss.

In any library you will find many books on inventions and inventors, and on mechanics, electricity, optics, and in fact just about anything you would want to know about in connection with whatever invention you are considering. And don't forget the encyclopedia. This is a good source for quick, condensed information.

About the Author

Harvey Weiss has written and illustrated many popular books for children, among them *Model Buildings and How to Make Them, How to Run a Railroad: Everything You Need to Know About Model Trains, Model Airplanes and How to Build Them, How to Make Your Own Books, Model Cars and Trucks and How to Build Them, Ship Models and How to Build Them,* and *Motors and Engines and How They Work.* A distinguished sculptor, whose work has received many awards and has been exhibited in galleries and museums across the country, he brings to his books a sure sense of what appeals to and can be accomplished by young people, and a sculptor's eye for simple, uncluttered forms.

A dedicated tinkerer and gadgeteer, he has exercised his considerable and varied skills in many different fields. Although his inventions range from the simplest device to the fairly elaborate, he will admit—with no guilt feelings whatsoever—that the great majority of his inventions are quite useless and were developed purely for the fun of it. His "Beckoning Machine" and his steam-propelled model airplane, both of which are described in this book, are typical of the sort of thing he enjoys most.

One of his current interests is the aesthetic aspects of machines and mechanical events. In a recent exhibition of his sculpture, several works had moving parts and might be described as part art, part invented machine.

Mr. Weiss is professor of sculpture at Adelphi University and lives in a much cluttered, much gadgeted old house in Greens Farms, Connecticut.